Text © 2012 by Jean Moss
Photographs © 2012 by Alexandra Grablewski
Illustrations © 2012 by The Taunton Press, Inc.
Charts & Schematics © 2012 by Jean Moss

All rights reserved.

The material was previously published in the book *Sweet Shawlettes: 25 Irresistible Patterns for Knitting Cowls, Capelets, and More* (ISBN 978-1-60085-400-2)
First published in this format 2013

The Taunton Press
Inspiration for hands-on living®

The Taunton Press, Inc., 63 South Main Street,
PO Box 5506, Newtown, CT 06470-5506
e-mail: tp@taunton.com

Cover design: Kimberly Adis
Interior design: Alison Wilkes
Illustrator: Jean Moss and Christine Erikson
Photographer: Alexandra Grablewski

Threads® is a trademark of The Taunton Press, Inc., registered in the U.S. Patent and Trademark Office.

The following names/manufacturers appearing in *Cable Shawlettes* are trademarks: Bergere de France®, Berroco®, Metallica FX®, Purelife®, Rowan®.
Standard Yarn weight System and Needle Hook Sizing information courtesy of the Craft Yarn Council, www.yarnstandards.com

Library of Congress Cataloging-in-Publication Data
Moss, Jean.
 Cable shawlettes : six original patterns to knit / Jean Moss.
   pages cm
  ISBN 978-1-62113-773-3 (pbk.)
1. Knitting--Patterns. 2. Knitwear. I. Title.
 TT825.M678 2013
 746.43'2041--dc23

Printed in the United States of America
10 9 8 7 6 5 4 3 2 1

Contents

Green at Heart Collar	2
Drift Cowl	6
Twine Cowl	8
Bess Ruff	12
Polperro Cape	16
Grace Cowl	20
Knitting Abbreviations	24
Needle and Hook Sizing	25
Standard Yarn Weight System	26
Techniques and Stitches	27
About the Author	29

Green at Heart Collar

Wear your eco-heart on your sleeve with this cozy collar, knitted in recycled wool so you can rest easy you're not adding to your carbon footprint. The pattern mixes cables and lace for a satisfying weekend project—perfect for those who like to be both stylish and sustainable!

SKILL LEVEL
Intermediate

FINISHED MEASUREMENTS
8 in. (20 cm) wide, 34½ in. (87.5 cm) long

YARN
Rowan Purelife® Renew
82 yd. (75 m) per 50 g ball:
3 balls Digger 682

NOTIONS
1 pair size 10 U.S. (6 mm) needles
or size to obtain gauge
Cable needle
Tapestry needle
3 buttons

GAUGE
18 sts and 20 rows = 4 in. (10 cm) in Green at Heart chart pattern (p. 5)

Note
Slip the first stitch and knit into the back of the last stitch on every row.

TO MAKE COLLAR
Cast on 38 sts and work in Moss St. for 1 in. (2.5 cm), ending on a WS row.
Buttonhole row (RS) Slip 1, k4, cast off 3 sts, k9, cast off 4 sts, k9, cast off 3 sts, k4, k1tbl.
Next row (WS) Work the Green at Heart Chart, starting on row 1, as follows:
Slip 1, work 36 sts of chart, k1tbl.
At the same time cast on over the cast-off sts when you come to them.
Work rows 1–19 of the chart in this manner, then rep from row 4 nine times (163 rows of chart); work row 1.
Work 1 in. (2.5 cm) in Moss St.
Cast off in pattern.

FINISHING
Weave in all ends securely using the tapestry needle.
Press lightly (p. 27) on the WS.
Attach 3 buttons opposite the buttonholes along the side edge of the Collar.

Create a completely different look by changing just the buttons, or try a solid yarn for fabulous stitch definition.

Green at Heart Chart

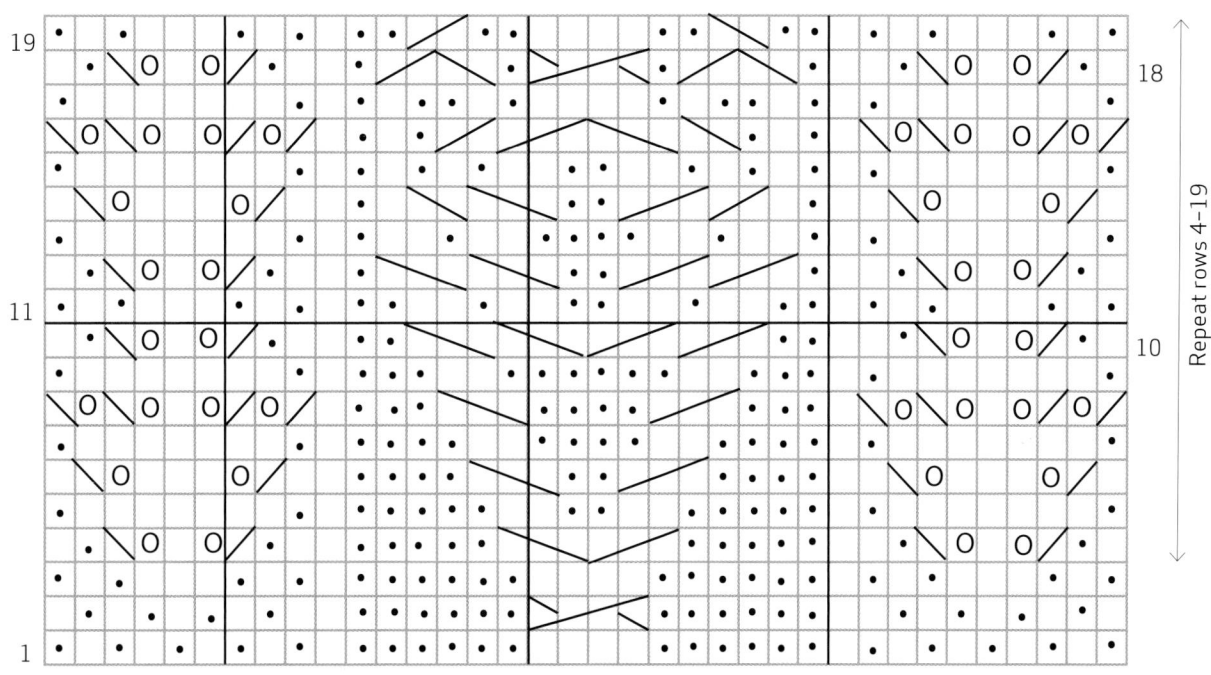

36 stitches

Note: Chart starts on WS row.

	K on RS, p on WS
•	P on RS, k on WS
╱	K2tog
╲	Ssk
O	Yo
	C2f—Slip 1 st to cn and hold at front, p1, k1 from cn.
	C2b—Slip 1 st to cn and hold at back, k1, p1 from cn.
	C3f—Slip 2 sts to cn and hold at front, p1, k2 from cn.
	C3b—Slip 1 st to cn and hold at back, k2, p1 from cn.
	C4f—Slip 2 sts to cn and hold at front, k2, k2 from cn.

Green at Heart Schematic

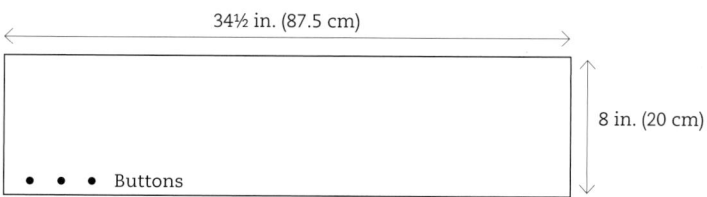

Drift Cowl

Don't be cowed by cables! This classy cowl is a great teacher and will have you cabling like a pro in no time—start it on a Friday evening and you'll wear it to work on Monday morning. With plenty of rest rows and virtually no finishing, you'll have spare time to find some fabulous buttons.

SKILL LEVEL
Easy

FINISHED MEASUREMENTS
8 in. (20 cm) wide, 28 in. (71 cm) long

YARN
Rowan Big Wool
87 yd. (80 m) per 100 g ball:
2 balls Vert 054

NOTIONS
1 pair size 17 U.S. (12 mm) needles
or size to obtain gauge
Cable needle
Size K-10½ U.S. (6.5 mm) crochet hook
Tapestry needle
3 buttons

GAUGE
13 sts and 13 rows = 4 in. (10 cm) in Cable Pattern

Note
For information on knitting cables, see p. 28.

Drift Schematic

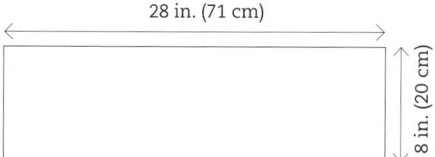

TO MAKE COWL
Cast on 26 sts and begin Cable Pattern (multiple of 12 sts).
Row 1 (Buttonhole row) Sl 1, k3, cast off 3 sts, k5, cast off 3 sts, k4, cast off 3 sts, k3, k1tbl.
Row 2 Sl 1, purl to last st, k1tbl, casting on over the cast-off sts as you come to them—26 sts.
Cont in Cable Pattern, beg on row 3 as follows (rows 1 and 2 have been worked already as buttonhole rows):
Row 1 Sl 1, knit to last st, k1tbl.
Row 2 Sl 1, purl to last st, k1tbl.
Row 3 Sl 1, *sl next 3 sts onto cn and hold at front of work, k3, k3 from cn, k6; rep from * to last st, k1tbl.
Row 4 Sl 1, purl to last st, k1tbl.
Row 5 Sl 1, knit to last st, k1tbl.
Row 6 Sl 1, purl to last st, k1tbl.
Row 7 Sl 1, *k6, sl next 3 sts to cn and hold at back of work, k3, k3 from cn; rep from * to last st, k1tbl.
Row 8 Sl 1, purl to last st, k1tbl.
Work all 8 rows of the Cable Pattern 11 times in all, then work rows 1–4 once—92 rows.
Work will measure approx 28 in. (71 cm) from the cast-on edge.
Cast off.

FINISHING
Work 1 row of single crochet at the cast-on and cast-off edges.
Securely weave in all ends.
Press lightly (p. 27) on the WS.
Neaten buttonholes and attach 3 buttons opposite the buttonholes along the cast-off edge.

Twine Cowl

This chunky cowl looks to the old craft of rope-making for its inspiration. Both abroad and closer to home, I've often watched fishermen on the quayside, mending nets, mooring their boats, raising sails—all activities dependent on rope. Traditionally, sailors have always sung shanties as they worked. Get in the groove with each of the three stitch patterns by creating a different song for each. Then you too can sing along as you knit!

SKILL LEVEL
Easy

FINISHED MEASUREMENTS
4 in. (10 cm) thick, approx 30 in. (76 cm) long

YARN
Rowan Big Wool
87 yd. (80 m) per 100 g ball:
2 balls each Linen 048 (A) and
Eternal 055 (C)
1 ball Concrete 061 (B)

NOTIONS
1 pair size 17 U.S. (12 mm) needles *or size to obtain gauge,* plus 1 extra needle
Cable needle
3 stitch holders
Tapestry needle

GAUGE
9 sts and 12 rows = 4 in. (10 cm) in Stockinette Stitch (p. 28)

Note
Slip the first stitch and knit into the back of the last stitch on every row.

TO MAKE COWL
Work approx 34 in. (86 cm) each in the Cable, Moss St., and Rib patterns in the color as instructed, leaving sts on holders.

Cable Pattern (1)
Using yarn (B) cast on 12 sts.
Row 1 Sl 1, knit to last st, k1tbl.
Row 2 Sl 1, purl to last st, k1tbl.
Row 3 Sl 1, slip next 5 sts onto cn and hold at front of work, k5, k5 from cn, k1tbl.
Rows 4, 6, 8, and 10 Sl 1, purl to last st, k1tbl.
Rows 5, 7, and 9 Sl 1, knit to last st, k1tbl.
Rep these 10 rows until the piece measures approx 34 in. (86 cm), ending on row 6. Place sts on holder.

Moss Stitch Pattern (2)
Using yarn (A), cast on 15 sts.
Row 1 Sl 1, *k1, p1; rep from * to last 2 sts, k1, k1tbl.
Rep row 1 to end. Place sts on holder.

Rib Pattern (3)

Using yarn (C), cast on 14 sts.
Row 1 Sl 1, *k2, p2; rep from * to last st, k1tbl.
Rep this row to end. Place sts on holder.

FINISHING

Using size 17 U.S. (12 mm) needles, place 15 sts of Moss St. pattern on a needle, then 12 sts of Cable pattern, and then 14 sts of Rib pattern—41 sts.
With RS facing, bring strand (C) over (B) and (A), finishing on the left of the pieces, then do the same in turn with strand (B) and strand (A), continuing until the Cowl is completely twisted, ending with yarn (C) on the RH side of the piece, as at top.
With RS facing, pick up and knit 41 sts across the bottom of the piece in the same order as the stitches on the needle at the top.
With RS together, work a Three-Needle Bind-Off using the extra needle, keeping colors correct.
Fold patterns 1 and 3 in half and arrange the cables to sit on the outside of the work. For extra stability, add sts here and there in the appropriate color yarn to secure.
Securely weave in ends.

Twine Schematic

Twist the three ends together.

| Moss St. Pattern 2 in (A) | Cable Pattern 1 in (B) | Rib Pattern 3 in (C) |

30 in. (76 cm) finished
34 in. (86.5 cm) before twisting

Twist patterns 3, 1, and 2 (respectively) over to the left until entire cowl is twisted, ending in the same position as shown.

It's all in the twist: The secret to Twine's wonderful, woven-rope look is the final step, which makes a rectangle into a twisting Möbius strip of alternating textures.

Thoughts on Color

Color has a powerful effect on our everyday lives. Here are some fun tips for choosing just the right color.

Red is a symbol of protection and caution in many cultures. It is powerful and passionate.

Blue is at once uplifting, relaxing, serene, and inspiring.

Yellow is the brightest color in the spectrum. It lifts the spirits and brings a sense of joy.

Green is nature's hallmark, said to encourage good fortune and healing.

Purple is a symbol of royalty, wealth, ritual, creativity, and eccentricity.

Neutrals such as ivory, taupe, and buff, borrow their hue from the natural world and are symbolic of wholeness and unity.

Metallics such as silver, gold, bronze, and copper bring life and oomph to the world around us, and in many cultures are thought to deflect the "evil eye" and inspire creativity.

Bess Ruff

The exquisite Tudor neck ruffs worn by Good Queen Bess inspired this striking design. The corrugated rib will get you up to speed for future Fair Isle projects, whilst the simple frill would add a touch of glamour to any scarf. Stylish and cozy, it stows away neatly in your purse—I won't be leaving home without mine this winter!

SKILL LEVEL
Intermediate

FINISHED MEASUREMENTS
16 in. (40.5 cm) wide, 5½ in. (14 cm) high

YARN
Rowan Silk Twist
93 yd. (85 m) per 50 g ball:
1 ball Ebony 671 (A)
1 ball Ruby 668 (B)

NOTIONS
1 pair size 6 U.S. (4 mm) needles
1 pair size 8 U.S. (5 mm) needles
or size to obtain gauge
Stitch markers
Tapestry needle
5 buttons

GAUGE
20 sts and 22 rows = 4 in. (10 cm) in Corrugated Rib

Notes
Slip the first stitch and knit into the back of the last stitch on every row.

TO MAKE RUFF
Using size 8 U.S. (5 mm) needles and yarn (A), cast on 78 sts and work in Corrugated Rib as follows:
Row 1 (RS) *K2 in (B), p2 in (A), rep from * to last 2 sts, k2 in (B).
Row 2 *P2 in (B), k2 in (A), rep from * to last 2 sts, p2 in (B).
Work as set until the piece measures 5 in. (12.75 cm), ending on a WS row.
Change to size 6 U.S. (4 mm) needles and yarn (A), cont in Stockinette St. to end:
Next row (RS) Knit into the front and back of every st—156 sts.
Next row Purl into the back and front of every st—312 sts.
Cast off using the picot point cast-off: Cast off 2 sts, *sl rem st on RH needle onto LH needle, cast on 1 st, cast off 3 sts; rep from * to end and fasten off rem st.

FINISHING
Button Band
Using size 6 U.S. (4 mm) needles and yarn (A), with RS facing, pick up and knit 23 sts along the top left side edge, below the frill, to the bottom of the side edge. Work 5 rows in Moss St. as follows:
Row 1 *K1, p1; rep from * to end.
Row 2 Purl the knit sts and knit the purl sts.
Rep row 2 three more times.
Cast off in Moss St.

Details such as lace edging and neat rows of little round buttons were hallmarks of Elizabethan dress, and give Bess old-fashioned charm.

Buttonhole Band

Work in the same way as button band, inserting 5 buttonholes on row 3 as follows: Mark the position of the 5 buttons on the button band so that the 1st and 5th buttons are marked 2 sts from each edge and the other 3 buttons are spaced evenly between.

Cast off 2 sts at each marker, casting them on again on the following row.

Attach the buttons opposite the buttonholes. To encourage the frill to stand up, thread the tapestry needle with yarn (A) and sew a small running st around the 1st row of frill. Pull the yarn tight until the frill fits the top of the Ruff, then securely fasten off.

Bess Schematic

16 in. (40.5 cm)

5½ in. (14 cm)

The Elizabethan Ruff

Queen Elizabeth I was a dedicated follower of fashion and dressed to impress. Clothes were an important status symbol for the Elizabethans, so the queen's attire had to be magnificent to outshine her courtiers. Neck ruffs, the intricate collars worn by both men and women of the time, became more and more elaborate as markers of social standing. These must-have pieces, kept in place using elaborate supports and underprops, framed the face and dictated the hairstyles of the period. Women's ruffs acquired a more feminine and seductive style by opening at the front to expose cleavage. With the introduction of starch in 1564, ruffs became ever more extravagant, and women's ruffs often were further decorated with lace, gold and silver threads, and fine silk. They sparkled with images of the sun, moon, and stars. The hugely expensive handmade lace or frilled fine linen needed to make a ruff ensured that only the wealthy could afford such an exquisite accessory.

Polperro Cape

The pretty Cornish village of Polperro, with its long knitting tradition, must have spawned many a gansey pattern. I like to imagine that the knitters there would appreciate this new take on their patterns. The denim yarn is hard wearing and gives great stitch definition as the color of the raised stitches starts to fade after a few washes. My wooden buckle complements the workwear look, but if you feel a Western moment coming on, a silver and turquoise buckle would add instant Navajo style.

SKILL LEVEL
Intermediate

FINISHED MEASUREMENTS
Approx 32 in. (81.5 cm) wide at shoulder, 14 in. (35.5 cm) long after washing

YARN
Rowan Denim
109 yd. (100 m) per 50 g ball:
6 balls Memphis 229
Yarn shrinks approx one-eighth in length when washed.

NOTIONS
1 pair size 3 U.S. (3.25 mm) needles
1 pair size 6 U.S. (4 mm) needles
or size to obtain gauge
Stitch markers
Tapestry needle
Buckle

GAUGE
24 sts and 32 rows = 4 in. (10 cm) in Polperro Chart pattern

TO MAKE CAPE
Using size 3 U.S. (3.25 mm) needles, cast on 70 sts and work 6 rows of Garter St.
Change to size 6 U.S. (4 mm) needles and begin working the Polperro Chart. Rep all 8 rows until the work measures approx 43 in. (109 cm) from the cast-on edge, ending on row 8.
Change to the smaller needles and work 6 rows in Garter St.
Cast off loosely.

Band
Using the smaller needles, cast on 25 sts and work as follows:
RS rows K12, p1, work sts 30–41 of the chart.
WS rows Work sts 30–41 of the chart, p13.
Keep cables, Stockinette St. (p. 121), and fold line sts correct as you knit.
Cont as set until the Band measures 41 in. (104 cm) from the cast-on edge, ending on either row 4 or row 8 of the chart pattern.
Cast off.

For an equally stunning wrap, choose cashmerino DK, work an extra 12 in. (30 cm) of the cable pattern, and omit the collar.

FINISHING

Sew a running stitch along the top edge of the Cape, gather until the edge measures 36 in. (91.5 cm), and secure.

Fold the Band in two along the fold line and slip-stitch cables to the facing at the cast-on and cast-off edges.

Starting at the left front edge, with the RS of the Cape facing the cabled edge of the Band, sew the Band to the Cape, leaving an extra 5 in. (12.7 cm) unsewn at the right front edge to go through the buckle.

To achieve given measurements, machine-wash the Cape in warm water, about 60°F (15.5°C), spin well, and tumble dry. Always wash the finished Cape separately.

Attach the buckle to the band at the left front edge.

Polperro Chart

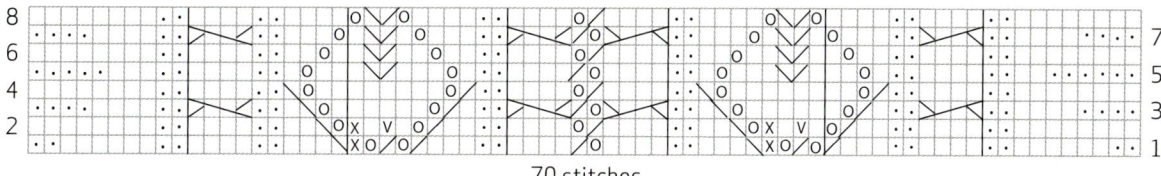

70 stitches

- □ K on RS, p on WS
- · P on RS, k on WS
- ╱ K2tog on RS, p2tog on WS
- O Yo
- X No stitch
- ╲ Ssk on RS, p2tog-b on WS
- V Inc 1—p1, p1-b in 1 st
- ⟋⟍ Sl 2 sts on cn and hold at back, k2, k2 from cn.
- ⟍⟋ Sl 2 sts on cn and hold at front, k2, k2 from cn.

Polperro Schematic

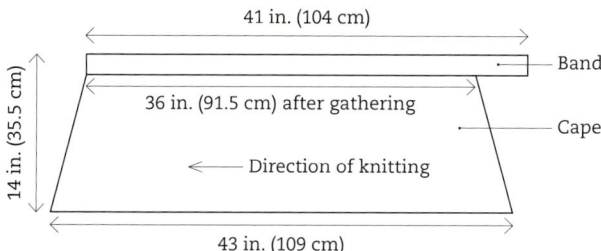

Note: Measurements before washing

Grace Cowl

Grace Kelly is the epitome of 1950s style. The Hermès scarves and Pringle twinsets she wore on her honeymoon with Prince Rainier became instant classics. I hope she would have approved of this delicate cowl, inspired by her cool, fragile elegance. It can be worn two ways—with the ruffled edge over the shoulders or, for a more flamboyant look, framing the face in a Tudor-style ruff. The simple drop-stitch rib pattern is distinctive yet discreet, allowing the glorious cashmere yarn to take center stage.

SKILL LEVEL
Intermediate

FINISHED MEASUREMENTS
7½ in. (19 cm) high, 18½ in. (47 cm) around at flat edge, 27 in. (68.5 cm) around at ruffled edge

YARN
Rowan Pure Cashmere DK
122 yd. (112 m) per 25 g ball:
2 balls Violetta 829

NOTIONS
Size 6 U.S. (4 mm) circular needle
or size to obtain gauge
Stitch marker
Tapestry needle

GAUGE
26 sts and 32 rows = 4 in. (10 cm) in Drop-Stitch Rib pattern

TO MAKE COWL
Cast on 120 sts loosely using the Cable Cast-On (p. 27). Place marker and join in the round, taking care not to twist the sts.
Work the Drop-Stitch Rib pattern, rep the 8 sts of pattern 15 times around, as follows:
Round 1 *P2, k1, yo, k1, p2, k2; rep from * around.
Rounds 2–6 *P2, k3, p2, k2; rep from * around.
Round 7 *P2, k1, drop next st and unravel down to yo of first round, k1, p2, k1, yo, k1; rep from * around.
Rounds 8–12 *P2, k2, p2, k3; rep from * around.
Round 13 *P2, k1, yo, k1, p2, k1, drop next st and unravel down to yo of 7th round, k1; rep from * around.
Rep from round 2.
Cont as set for 49 rounds; on the final round, omit the yarn overs.
Work 2 rounds keeping the 2 by 2 rib pattern correct.
Next round *P1, yo, p1, k1, yo, k1; rep from * around.
Next round *P3, k3; rep from * around.
Rep the last round until the work measures 7½ in. (19 cm).

Next round *P1, drop next st and unravel down to yo of 52nd round, p1, k1, drop next st and unravel down to yo of 52nd round, yo, k1; rep from * around.

Cast off knitwise using the picot point cast-off: Cast off 2 sts, *slip rem st from RH needle onto the LH needle, cast on 2 sts, cast off 4 sts; rep from * to end and fasten off rem st.

FINISHING

Using the tapestry needle, weave in ends securely on the WS.

Press lightly (p. 27) on the WS.

Grace Schematic

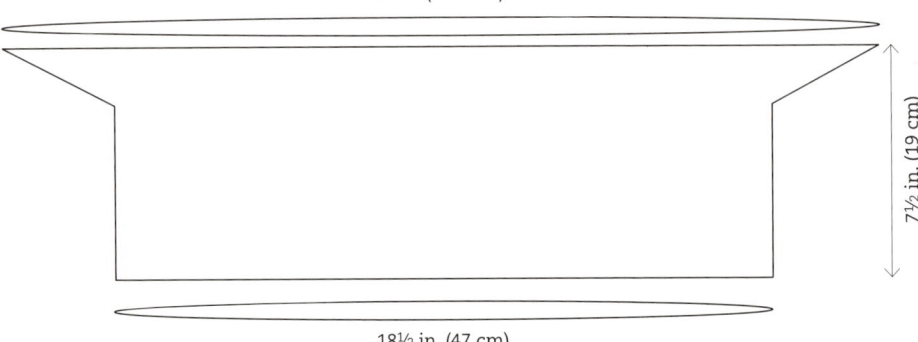

If your budget doesn't run to cashmere, try a mercerized cotton—soft and silky, with the bonus of cotton's perfect stitch definition.

Knitting Abbreviations

alt   alternate
approx   approximately
beg   beginning
ch   chain (single crochet)
cm   centimeter(s)
cn   cable needle
cont   continue
dec   decrease
ev   every
g   gram(s)
in.   inch(es)
inc   increase
k   knit
k2tog   knit 2 sts together
k3tog   knit 3 sts together
kfb   knit st in front and back
kwise   knitwise
LH   left hand
m   meter(s)
mm   millimeter(s)
p   purl
p2tog   purl 2 sts together
p2tog-b   p1, return this st to LH needle, then with point of RH needle, pass next st over and off needle; then slip st back to RH needle

p3tog   purl 3 sts together
pm   place marker
psso   pass slipped st over
rep   repeat
rem   remaining
RH   right hand
RS   right side
s2kpo   sl2tog kwise, k1, pass 2 slipped sts over
sk   skip
sk2po   slip 1 st wyib, k2tog, psso
skpo   slip 1 st, k1, pass the slipped st over
sl   slip
sl2tog   slip 2 sts together
ssk   (slip, slip, knit)—slip next 2 sts knitwise, one at a time, to RH needle. Insert tip of LH needle into fronts of these sts from left to right and knit them together.
st(s)   stitch(es)
tbl   through back loop
tog   together
w & t   wrap yarn and turn work
WS   wrong side
wyib   with yarn in back
yd.   yard(s)
yo   yarn over needle to make 1 st

Needle and Hook Sizing

Knitting Needles

Millimeter Range	U.S. Size Range
2.25 mm	1
2.75 mm	2
3.25 mm	3
3.5 mm	4
3.75 mm	5
4 mm	6
4.5 mm	7
5 mm	8
5.5 mm	9
6 mm	10
6.5 mm	10½
8 mm	11
9 mm	13
10 mm	15
12.75 mm	17
15 mm	19
19 mm	35
25 mm	50

Crochet Hooks

Millimeter Range	U.S. Size Range
2.25 mm	B-1
2.75 mm	C-2
3.25 mm	D-3
3.5 mm	E-4
3.75 mm	F-5
4 mm	G-6
4.5 mm	7
5 mm	H-8
5.5 mm	I-9
6 mm	J-10
6.5 mm	K-10½
8 mm	L-11
9 mm	M/N-13
10 mm	N/P-15
15 mm	P/Q
16 mm	Q
19 mm	S

Standard Yarn Weight System

Yarn Weight Symbol and Category Name	Super Fine 1	Fine 2	Light 3	Medium 4	Bulky 5	Super Bulky 6
Types of yarn in category	Sock, fingering, baby	Sport, baby	DK, light worsted	Worsted, afghan, Aran	Chunky, craft, rug	Bulky, roving
Knit gauge range in St st in 4 in.*	27–32 sts	23–26 sts	21–24 sts	16–20 sts	12–15 sts	6–11 sts
Recommended metric needle size	2.25–3.25 mm	3.25–3.75 mm	3.75–4.5 mm	4.5–5.5 mm	5.5–8 mm	8 mm and larger
Recommended U.S. needle size	1–3	3–5	5–7	7–9	9–11	11 and larger
Crochet gauge range in sc in 4 in.*	21–31 sts	16–20 sts	12–17 sts	11–14 sts	8–11 sts	5–9 sts
Recommended metric hook size	2.25–3.5 mm	3.5–4.5 mm	4.5–5.5 mm	5.5–6.5 mm	6.5–9 mm	9 mm and larger
Recommended U.S. hook size	B/1–E/4	E/4–7	7–I/9	I/9–K/10.5	K/10.5–M/13	M/13 and larger

*The information in this table reflects the most commonly used gauges and needle or hook sizes for the specific yarn categories.

Techniques and Stitches

Backward Loop Cast-On
This simple cast-on is useful for casting on stitches in the middle of a row. It's sometimes used for making a stitch between stitches.

Make a backward loop and place it on the needle. Repeat as many times as required.

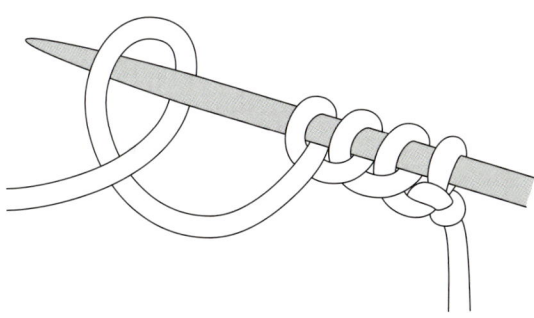

Cable Cast-On
This is a useful cast-on when stitches need to be added within your work.

Make a slip knot on the LH needle. Working into this knot's loop, k1 st and place it on the LH needle.

Insert the RH needle between the last 2 sts. From this position, k1 st and place it on the LH needle. Rep this step to cast on each additional st.

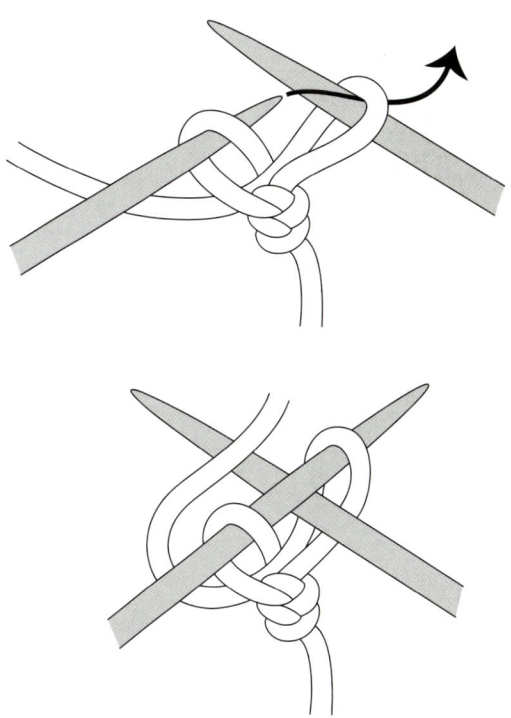

Blocking and Pressing
Never underestimate the power of blocking and pressing! Small mistakes often become invisible when a piece is well presented. Some projects need pressing more than others, so I've included specific instructions to press in some projects.

Before blocking, neaten the selvages by sewing or weaving in all the ends along the sides or along color joins where appropriate. Then, using pins, block each piece of knitting to shape—this also gives you an opportunity to check the measurements. Gently press each piece on the WS, omitting ribbing, using a warm iron and a damp pressing cloth. Take special care with the edges.

Cables

Cabling is a simply a way of crossing one set of stitches over another set and looks best when worked against a contrasting background stitch, like working a Stockinette Stitch cable on a reverse Stockinette Stitch background. Basic cables are worked by placing the first set of stitches on a cable needle and holding them at the back or front of your knitting, depending on whether you want the crossing to slope toward the right or left. Holding the stitches at the front will result in a left-sloping cable, and holding them at the back will yield a right-sloping cable. For example, here's a 4-stitch cable that slopes to the left:

On a RS row, work to the position of the cable and sl the next 2 sts onto the cable needle, holding it at the *front* of the work.

Working behind the cable needle, knit the next 2 sts from the LH needle.

Now knit the 2 sts from the cable needle to create a crossover to the left.

Chart Reading

When knitting back and forth, charts are read from right to left on RS rows and from left to right on WS rows. Charts can begin with a RS or WS row; this will be indicated by where Row 1 is situated on the chart. For instance, if Row 1 is on the left, then the chart starts with a WS row, if it is on the right, it starts with a RS row. In circular knitting, all rows are RS rows and every row is read from right to left.

Every square (or rectangle) in a chart represents 1 stitch horizontally and 1 row vertically. The symbols inside each square represent either stitches (knit, purl, cable, and so on) or colors (in intarsia or two-color stranded knitting). When working with several colors, it's good to tape a small piece of each color alongside its symbol so you have a constant reminder of which yarn to use.

To keep track of your place in the chart, use a premade line finder or make one yourself by taking a strip of card or plastic the width of the chart and cut a long slit into it, approximately the size of a row. This window can then be moved up the chart as you knit, masking the rows you've knitted and highlighting the one you're working on. If the size of a chart is too small for comfortable reading as printed in the book, enlarge it using a photocopier before you start the project.

Stockinette Stitch

Knit on RS rows and purl on WS rows.

Stockinette Stitch in the Round

Knit every round.

About the Author

JEAN MOSS IS ONE OF Britain's leading knit designers. Her innovative combinations of intricate textures, striking colorways, and sophisticated styling have been widely influential in the global knitting community.

A self-taught knitwear designer, Jean produced her own unique collections of handknits for many years, which were sold in the United States, Japan, and Europe. In the 1980s and 1990s, Jean also worked on design and production for many international fashion houses, such as Polo Ralph Lauren, Laura Ashley, and Benetton. Currently, her designs are featured regularly in *Rowan Knitting and Crochet Magazine, The Knitter*, and *Vogue Knitting,* and for six years she hosted "Ask Jean," an advice column in the U.K. magazine *Knitting*.

Jean is passionate about good design and has always believed that it should be available to all who appreciate it, not just the few who can afford to buy couture. *Sweet Shawlettes* is her 10th book of handknit designs, the most recent being *In The Mood* and *Wandering Spirits* for Araucania Yarns.

Jean's other passions include gardening, music, and vegetarian food. Her personal take on color, texture, shape, and form is expressed in the one-off, imaginative gardens she designs for clients in North Yorkshire, England. Music plays a big part in her life, and her album *More Yarn Will Do the Trick* is a trio of textile-related songs.

For the past decade, Jean and her partner, Philip, have hosted knitting and garden tours in the United Kingdom, which have become so successful that they are now going further afield to exotic locations such as Morocco and Greece. She loves to meet other knitters and travels extensively, teaching workshops in both the United States and Europe. For more information on Jean's books, patterns, kits, ready-to-wear, workshops, lectures, and tours, visit www.jeanmoss.com.

Look for these other *Threads* Selects booklets at www.taunton.com and wherever crafts are sold.

Baby Beanies
Debby Ware
EAN: 9781621137634
8 ½ x 10 ⅞, 32 pages
Product# 078001
$9.95 U.S., $11.95 Can.

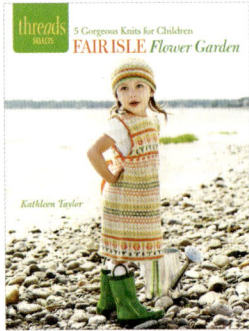

Fair Isle Flower Garden
Kathleen Taylor
EAN: 9781621137702
8 ½ x 10 ⅞, 32 pages
Product# 078008
$9.95 U.S., $11.95 Can.

Fair Isle Hats, Scarves, Mittens & Gloves
Kathleen Taylor
EAN: 9781621137719
8 ½ x 10 ⅞, 32 pages
Product# 078009
$9.95 U.S., $11.95 Can.

Lace Socks
Kathleen Taylor
EAN: 9781621137894
8 ½ x 10 ⅞, 32 pages
Product# 078012
$9.95 U.S., $11.95 Can.

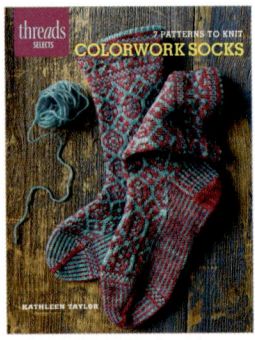

Colorwork Socks
Kathleen Taylor
EAN: 9781621137740
8 ½ x 10 ⅞, 32 pages
Product# 078011
$9.95 U.S., $11.95 Can.

DIY Bride Cakes & Sweets
Khris Cochran
EAN: 9781621137665
8 ½ x 10 ⅞, 32 pages
Product# 078004
$9.95 U.S., $11.95 Can.

DIY Bride Beautiful Bouquets
Khris Cochran
EAN: 9781621137672
8 ½ x 10 ⅞, 32 pages
Product# 078005
$9.95 U.S., $11.95 Can.

Bead Necklaces
Susan Beal
EAN: 9781621137641
8 ½ x 10 ⅞, 32 pages
Product# 078002
$9.95 U.S., $11.95 Can.

Drop Earrings
Susan Beal
EAN: 9781621137658
8 ½ x 10 ⅞, 32 pages
Product# 078003
$9.95 U.S., $11.95 Can.

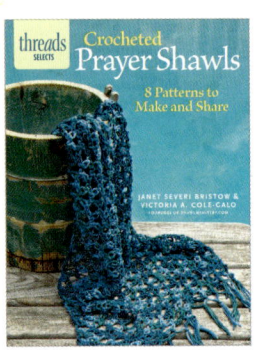

Crocheted Prayer Shawls
Janet Severi Bristow &
Victoria A. Cole-Galo
EAN: 9781621137689
8 ½ x 10 ⅞, 32 pages
Product# 078006
$9.95 U.S., $11.95 Can.

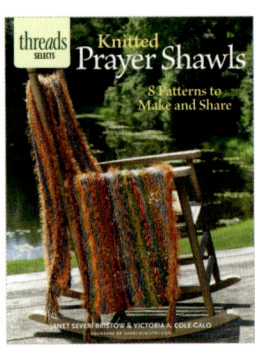

Knitted Prayer Shawls
Janet Severi Bristow &
Victoria A. Cole-Galo
EAN: 9781621137696
8 ½ x 10 ⅞, 32 pages
Product# 078007
$9.95 U.S., $11.95 Can.

Shawlettes
Jean Moss
EAN: 9781621137726
8 ½ x 10 ⅞, 32 pages
Product# 078010
$9.95 U.S., $11.95 Can.

Look for these other *Threads* Selects booklets at www.taunton.com and wherever crafts are sold.

Easy-to-Sew Flowers
EAN: 9781621138259
8 ½ x 10 ⅞, 32 pages
Product# 078017
$9.95 U.S., $9.95 Can.

Easy-to-Sew Gifts
EAN: 9781621138310
8 ½ x 10 ⅞, 32 pages
Product# 078023
$9.95 U.S., $9.95 Can.

Easy-to-Sew Handbags
EAN: 9781621138242
8 ½ x 10 ⅞, 32 pages
Product# 078016
$9.95 U.S., $9.95 Can.

Easy-to-Sew Kitchen
EAN: 9781621138327
8 ½ x 10 ⅞, 32 pages
Product# 078024
$9.95 U.S., $9.95 Can.

Easy-to-Sew Lace
EAN: 9781621138228
8 ½ x 10 ⅞, 32 pages
Product# 078014
$9.95 U.S., $9.95 Can.

Easy-to-Sew Lingerie
EAN: 9781621138235
8 ½ x 10 ⅞, 32 pages
Product# 078015
$9.95 U.S., $9.95 Can.

Easy-to-Sew Pet Projects
EAN: 9781621138273
8 ½ x 10 ⅞, 32 pages
Product# 078018
$9.95 U.S., $9.95 Can.

Easy-to-Sew Pillows
EAN: 9781621138266
8 ½ x 10 ⅞, 32 pages
Product# 078019
$9.95 U.S., $9.95 Can.

Easy-to-Sew Scarves & Belts
EAN: 9781621138211
8 ½ x 10 ⅞, 32 pages
Product# 078013
$9.95 U.S., $9.95 Can.

Easy-to-Sew Skirts
EAN: 9781621138280
8 ½ x 10 ⅞, 32 pages
Product# 078020
$9.95 U.S., $9.95 Can.

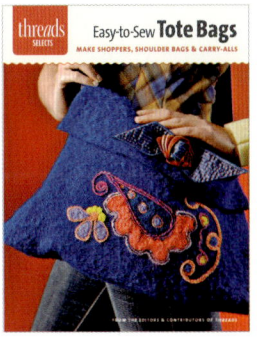

Easy-to-Sew Tote Bags
EAN: 9781621138297
8 ½ x 10 ⅞, 32 pages
Product# 078021
$9.95 U.S., $9.95 Can.

Easy-to-Sew Windows
EAN: 9781621138303
8 ½ x 10 ⅞, 32 pages
Product# 078022
$9.95 U.S., $9.95 Can.

If you like these projects, you'll love these books by Jean Moss:

Sweet Shawlettes
25 irresistible patterns for knitting cowls, capelets, and more

Jean Moss

A wonderfully creative collection of 25 knitting patterns for shawlettes, mini-wraps, cowls, collars, and more. The garments are grouped by style: Country, Couture, Folk, and Vintage and feature gorgeous yarns, including wool, silk, cotton, and sustainable fibers. Knitters of all levels will draw inspiration from the gorgeous four-color photos. Additionally helpful are illustrations, charts, schematics and an appendix with instructions for special stitches.

Paperback, Product #071355, $21.95 U.S.

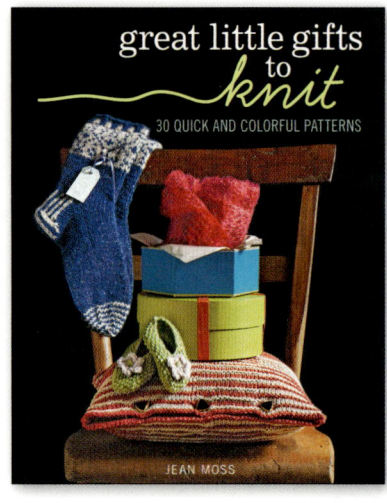

Great Little Gifts to Knit
30 quick and colorful patterns

Jean Moss

In a weekend, or less, you can make any one of these 30 quick-and-easy knitting gifts. This upbeat guide features fun, fresh, beautiful patterns that incorporate traditional knitting techniques from all over the world: from Fair Isle and Aran knits to Peruvian intarsia patterns and Japanese shadow knitting techniques. Beautiful, clever, and, most of all, quick to knit, these projects offer knitters a chance to learn and experiment with new techniques—all in projects that can be made in two days or less.

Paperback, Product #071445, $21.95 U.S.

Shop for these and other great craft books online: www.tauntonstore.com

Simply search by product number or call 800-888-8286, use code MX800126

Call Monday-Friday 9AM - 9PM EST and Saturday 9AM - 5PM EST • International customers, call 203-702-2204